Guaranteed Formula for Writing

Effective Business Emails & Letters

by Everett Ofori, MBA (UK), MSF (USA)

Guaranteed Formula for Writing Effective Business Emails & Letters

ISBN 10: 1-894221-06-0
ISBN 13: 978-1-894221-06-1

Author contact: everettoforijapan@gmail.com
               www.everettofori.com

As soon as you move one step from the bottom,
your effectiveness depends on your ability
to reach others through
the spoken or written word.

- Dr. Peter F. Drucker
Management Consultant, Professor, Author

✳✳✳

...though anyone can learn to write effectively, it takes hard work...writing is like any other skill — you can improve, but you'll have to dedicate yourself to it. The easier path is to settle for being a so-so writer...If you can write — really write — people will assume certain other things about you, the most important is that you're a clear thinker.

- Bryan A. Garner
Author & Distinguished Research Professor of Law
Southern Methodist University, USA

Other books by Everett Ofori

1) Succeeding From the Margins of Canadian Society: A Strategic Resource for New Immigrants, Refugees and International Students. Written by Francis Adu-Febiri and Everett Ofori© 2009 – ISBN 978-1-926585-27-7

2) Read Assure: Guaranteed Formula for Reading Success with Phonics. © 2010 – ISBN 978-1894221054

3) Guaranteed Formula for Writing Success. © 2019 – ISBN 978-1-926918-22-8

4) The Changing Japanese Woman: From Yamatonadeshiko to YamatonadeGucci   © 2013 – ISBN 13: 978-1894221047

5) Prepare for Greatness: How to Make Your Success Inevitable. © 2013 – ISBN 13: 978-0921143000

6) The Global Student's Companion: 10,001 Timeless Themes & Topics for Dialogue, Discussion & Debate Practice. Compiled by Everett Ofori   © 2015 – ISBN 13: 978-1-894221-02-3

7) Guaranteed Formula for Effective Business Writing. © 2011 – ISBN 978-1894221108

8) Guaranteed Formula for Public Speaking Success. © 2011 – ISBN 978-1894221078

9) 3,570 Real-world English Phrases for Speaking & Writing Practice (Volume 1) © 2011 – ISBN 978-1894221125

10) 3,570 Real-world English Phrases for Speaking & Writing Practice (Volume 2) © 2011 – ISBN 978-1894221139

IF YOU CAN THINK WELL, PLAN WELL, WRITE WELL, AND SPEAK WELL,
YOU HAVE ALL THAT YOU NEED TO CHANGE THE COURSE OF HUMAN HISTORY,
OR AT LEAST, YOUR OWN HISTORY.

-Everett Ofori

Simple English is no one's mother tongue.
It has to be worked for.
- Jacques Barzun, American writer & educator

Important Note:

Guaranteed Formula for Writing Effective Business Emails & Letters has been spun off an earlier book, _Guaranteed Formula for Effective Business Writing_, to benefit those who just want to focus on emails and letters rather than proposals and reports.

Table of contents   **Page**

Acknowledgments

Thanks very much to Ms Diana Camargo and Mr Frank Pridgen, who provided suggestions for improvement of the text. I am also grateful to all the instructors who have used this book in their classes and provided feedback on their experience. Special thanks to Mr Warren Buffett of Berkshire Hathaway, USA, for granting me permission to use an excerpt from one of his annual letters as an example. Students who have used this book have also provided invaluable feedback. Thanks.

- Everett Ofori, Tokyo, Japan

NOTE TO INSTRUCTOR & STUDENT

The instructor's role is to review the student's work for content, format, organization, and grammar. For best results, students should get in the habit of drafting their work, and then, reviewing the work themselves for common errors before submitting it to the instructor. The instructor checks the work and makes suggestions, pointing out areas of weakness and strength. The student might be encouraged to write another draft that incorporates the instructor's suggestions.

The author highly recommends that this book be used in conjunction with an English grammar book so that the student can be fully immersed both in the review of grammar and the practice of writing.

FOR CLASSROOM USE

The material in this book has been successfully used in the classroom. Some students only have time for writing practice during class. Such students may read the material at home and do the exercises in class or read and write in class. Of course, it is also possible for the student to do both the reading and writing at home and meet the instructor for discussion and feedback. Ample space has been provided in this book for writing practice.

Preface

Writing is a bit like swimming. You can imagine yourself swimming like an eel or diving to the bottom of the ocean like an octopus, but if you never get yourself wet, if you never experience both the dread and exhilaration of cutting through the water, you'll never be the swimmer of your dreams. If you want to be a good writer, you have to write...a lot...and get feedback from someone with the relevant knowledge and experience...and then write again... and again. It is the same formula that great writers such as Hemingway used to make their mark. Your goal may simply be to write polished letters and emails, but as with Hemingway, you will profit from repeated practice.

Here's an excerpt of an interview given by the Nobel Prize winning writer, Ernest Hemingway.

Interviewer: How much rewriting do you do?
Hemingway: It depends. I rewrote the ending of *Farewell to Arms*, the last page of it, thirty-nine times.
Interviewer: Was there some technical problem there? What was it that had stumped you?
Hemingway: Getting the words right.

Even for Hemingway, a native speaker of English and a writer besides, clear, powerful, and effective sentences did not come by magic. He had to work at it.

It might interest you, then, to know that this book provides over 170 writing-related assignments comprising emails, letters, reports, proposals, and sentence construction.

~~~~~~~~~~~~

Write. Rewrite. When not writing or rewriting, read.
I know of no other shortcuts.

- Larry L. King (U.S.A.), playwright, journalist, and novelist

Indispensable Writers' Resources

Dictionary

Make it a habit to check and confirm the meanings of words. Some online dictionaries such as **www.merriamwebster.com** include an audio pronunciation link. You can thus benefit not only from knowing the meaning of a word but also how it is pronounced. Another dictionary that comes highly recommended is the Oxford English Dictionary.

Thesaurus

You also need to have access to a thesaurus, which gives you words of similar meaning . In fact, the online Merriam Webster dictionary includes a thesaurus that gives you both synonyms and antonyms.

One should be careful, however, in using a thesaurus because even though words may have similar meanings, often, they carry different connotations. So, choose your words carefully. If possible, the writer should confirm the specific meaning of an unfamiliar word before using it.

Usage books

Books on usage often focus on some of the more confusing words in the language. For example, what is the difference between preparation and preparedness? And what is the difference between continual and continuous?

Because of the similarity in the pronunciation or spelling of certain pairs of words, they are frequently misused or misapplied. Usage books aim to help writers make better choices about words and phrases.

Perhaps, the best known book of usage is *Fowler's Modern English Usage*. Others include John Sinclair's *Collins Cobuild English Usage*, and Michael Swan's *Practical English Usage*.

Reference Phrases...If Need Be

The following reference phrases will help you to understand the patterns of language usually used in letter writing and emails. Use them only as a guide. Once you've come to understand the drift of English email and letter writing, let the issue before you dictate how you write the letter. Do not become a copy-and-paste writer. This book shows you a better way.

Salutation & Complimentary Close
(When you do not know the name of the person you are writing to)

Dear Customer,

    Yours faithfully,

Dear Editor,

    Yours faithfully,

Dear Sir,

    Yours faithfully,

Dear Madam,

    Yours faithfully,

Dear Sir or Madam,

    Yours faithfully,

Salutation & Complimentary Close
(When you know the name of the person you are writing to)

Dear Mrs[1] Roxbart,

        Yours sincerely,

Dear Mr Kobayashi,

        Yours sincerely,

Dear Mrs Widodo,

        Yours sincerely,

Dear Ms Thaber,

        Yours sincerely,

Salutation & Complimentary Close
(When you are writing to a good friend)

Dear Eva,

        Best wishes,

Ray,

        Best wishes,

Hi Sandra,

        Best wishes

Hello Marcus,

        Best wishes

---

1 You may put a period after titles (Mr. / Ms. / Mrs.). If you decide to do so, be consistent throughout. Don't use the period sometimes and omit it at times. Likewise, if you decide not to insert the period, then refrain from doing so throughout your document.

Greetings at the Start of a Letter (A Warm Opening)

- I hope all is well with you.

- I hope you are enjoying the fine weather.

- I hope you and yours are doing great at this time of year.

- How are you? I trust all is well.

Requests / Inquiries

More formal	Less formal
I would be grateful if you could...	Could you please...?
I would appreciate it if you could...	Could you possibly....?
I would be most grateful if you could send me...	Send me...
I would be most grateful if you would...	Do me a favor, will you?
Would you be so kind as to...	Would it be possible for you to...?
I was wondering if you could...	I need...
Would it be possible for you to...	Could I ask you to...?

I am interested in...
> - *I am interested in the blue diamond that you advertised in the classified section of GemBright Times.*

I was interested in finding out...
> - *I was interested in finding out if the blue diamond that you advertised is still available for sale.*

I understand that your company specializes in...
> - *I understand that your company specializes in blue diamonds; I would like to obtain information about your products, including terms of delivery.*

I would be most grateful if you...
> *- I would be most grateful if you would consider visiting our booth at the Milan Precious Stones trade fair in July, 20XX.*

I am writing with reference to your advertisement...
> *- I am writing with reference to your advertisement in the Japan Herald of November 7, 20XX, for the services of a plumber. I am a highly experienced plumber.*

Responding to Requests / Inquiries / Orders

Thank you for your letter of [DATE].
> *- Thank you for your letter of August 1, 20XX.*

Thanks very much for your enquiry of [DATE].
> *- Thanks very much for your enquiry of September 17, 20XX.*

I was happy to learn of your interest in...
> *- I was happy to learn of your interest in our range of products.*

Thanks very much for your enquiry dated November 7, 20XX, in which you...
> *- Thanks very much for your enquiry dated November 7, 20XX, in which you requested a copy of our latest price list.*

We are pleased to inform you that...
> *- We are pleased to inform you that the product you inquired about is still in stock.*

It was a pleasure to receive your order for...
> *- It was a pleasure to receive your order for 30 cases of Honey-Badger Cocoa drink.*

Thank you for your enquiry of [DATE], regarding...
> *- Thank you for your enquiry of August 7, 20XX, regarding stylish mobile phone cases.*

We recently received a request from you regarding...
> - *We recently received a request from you regarding steel-rimmed tennis rackets.*

With reference to your enquiry of...
> - *With reference to your enquiry of July 2, 20XX, we have enclosed a product list and related prices.*

Our company specializes in the products you are looking for. We have therefore enclosed...
> - *Our company specializes in the products you are looking for. We have therefore enclosed details of our full range of products and their prices.*

We are delighted to...
> - *We are delighted to send you a copy of our latest catalog.*

Close (request-related)

We look forward to developing...
> - *We look forward to developing a mutually beneficial business relationship.*

It would be our pleasure to provide you with...
> - *It would be our pleasure to provide you with any further information you might need.*

You can be sure that...
> - *You can be sure that we will attend to all your orders promptly.*

Kindly let me know...
> - *Kindly let me know if you need any further information.*

We trust you will find...
> - *We trust you will find our quotation satisfactory and look forward to hearing from you again shortly.*

Asking for Help

Could you...(for me)?

> - *Could you prepare the report for me by Friday, November 7, 20XX?*

Would you please...?

> - *Would you please let me know how the deal went?*

Would you mind (verb+ing)...?

> - *Would you mind **coming** to the 14th floor, Room 1407, this afternoon for a meeting?*

Could you possibly...?

> - *Could you possibly do a presentation some time next week on the research you have been working on?*

Would it be all right...

> - *Would it be all right if the sales team held its weekly meeting in Room 5 this week instead of Room 10.*

I wonder if...

> - *I wonder if I can borrow one of your trucks to move some goods from Buffalo, N.Y. to Toronto, Canada.*

Possible Responses to Requests for Help

Okay, no problem.	(informal)
Sure, I'd be glad to.	(informal)
Sorry, I'm busy right now.	(semi-formal)
I'm sorry. I don't have time right now.	(semi-formal)
I'm afraid I am unable to fulfill your request right now.	(formal)
I would be happy to accede to your request.	(formal)
It would be my pleasure to implement the program.	(formal)

Following a Phone Call

As we discussed on the telephone, here is...
> - *As we discussed on the telephone, here is the price list you asked for.*

We were happy to receive your phone call yesterday. The...
> - *We were happy to receive your phone call yesterday. The products you asked about are now in stock.*

In response to your telephone call...
> - *In response to your telephone call, we are happy to offer you a small discount.*

Bad News Letter

After careful consideration...
> - *After careful consideration, we regret to inform you that we would have to withdraw our sponsorship of your soccer team, the Incredibles.*

Unfortunately, your request for...
> - *Unfortunately, your request for special privileges to use the office from 1 a.m. to 4 a.m. is denied.*

Unfortunately, we cannot...
> - *Unfortunately, we cannot grant you a raise at this time.*

Unfortunately, we are not in a position to...
> - *Unfortunately, we are not in a position to extend the contract for your cleaning service into the next fiscal year.*

We regret to inform you that...
> - *We regret to inform you that your application for a subsidy has been denied.*

I'm sorry, but...
> - *I'm sorry, but we cannot accept the terms you offered.*

Good News Letter

I am happy to say that...

> *- I am happy to say that your application for admission to our three-month Executive Management course has been approved.*

We are delighted to inform you that...

> *- We are delighted to inform you that your proposal for expansion of your territory has been accepted.*

Expressing Sympathy and Condolences

It was with deep regret that we heard...

> *- It was with deep regret that we heard of the death of your Chief Marketing Officer, Ms Lelani Delacroix.*

I wish to extend our deepest sympathy on...

> *- I wish to extend our deepest sympathy on the loss of your son, Brian Busby.*

Please accept our sincere condolences on...

> *- Please accept our sincere condolences on the passing of your mother, Mrs Laoko Brobbey.*

We were very sad to hear...

> *- We were very sad to hear of the passing of your uncle, Mr Ronald Bokushi.*

We were very sorry to hear...

> *- We were very sorry to hear that your grandfather passed away last week.*

Apology Letters

I am writing to apologize for...
> - *I am writing to apologize for the delay in processing your order.*

We are very sorry that...
> - *We are very sorry that you received the wrong order from us.*

I'd like to apologize for...
> - *I'd like to apologize for the delay in processing your order.*

I'm sorry about...
> - *I'm sorry about the way our staff treated you and your family at our restaurant the other day.*

I'm sorry that...
> - *I'm sorry that no one attended to you for thirty minutes when you visited our office last Friday.*

I'm very sorry for...
> - *I'm sorry for the rude treatment of your grandparents at our establishment last week.*

Please accept my apologies.
> - *What happened to you last week in our office was an isolated incident.* ***Please accept my apologies.***

Please accept my sincere apologies.
> - *Having to wait for so long for service is against everything we stand for.* ***Please accept my sincere apologies*** *and be assured that it will never happen again.*

Please forgive me for...
> - *Please forgive me for the repeated mispronunciation of your name.*

Asking for Information

I am writing to ask about...

> *- I am writing to ask about the new training program you have created for new managers.*

I am writing to enquire about...

> *- I am writing to enquire about your volunteering opportunities.*

I would like to know if...

> *- I would like to know if I can take part in your art program.*

Complaining

I'm writing to complain about...

> *- I'm writing to complain about the way I was treated in your flagship store on Orville Road last Thursday, February 22, 20XX.*

I'm writing to express dissatisfaction about...

> *- I'm writing to express dissatisfaction about the lack of air conditioning on your train from A to B on December 8, 20XX.*

I was very disappointed about...

> *- I was very dissapointed about your misplaced attack on my secretary last Friday.*

I am not happy about...

> *- I am not happy about the long, unproductive meetings.*

I am not happy with...

> *- I am not happy with the long breaks some of you are taking.*

Asking for Payment

Please see attached...
> - *Please see attached an invoice for services rendered to your firm between February 7, 20XX and February 28, 20XX.*

We have enclosed our invoice for...
> - *We have enclosed our invoice for services provided to your company in June 20XX.*

Our enclosed invoice shows that a balance of...
> - *Our enclosed invoice shows that a balance of ¥15,000 remains to be paid.*

We would be most grateful...
> - *We would be most grateful if you could send payment in the amount of $3,023.00 immediately.*

Acknowledging Payment

We have received your payment of [AMOUNT] for [PRODUCT/SERVICE].
> - *We have received your payment of $450.00 for services rendered in January 20XX.*

Thanks very much for sending payment...
> - *Thanks very much for sending payment in the amount of $750.00 for the matrix-style solar lantern.*

Payment / Reminders / Collection Letters

We hope you can send the funds...
> - *We hope you can send the funds by the end of this month.*

This is just a reminder...
> - *This is just a reminder that your payment for the piano is past due.*

We would appreciate hearing from you...
> - *We would appreciate hearing from you regarding a possible payment plan.*

This is a friendly reminder that...
> - *This is a friendly reminder that your payment for the scooter is due.*

Please let us hear from you by...
> - *Please let us hear from you by December 2, 20XX.*

Congratulating Others

Congratulations on...[OCCASION]
> - *Congratulations on winning a scholarship to attend the International Business Management Institute's program on negotiation.*

> - *Congratulations on your company's 10th anniversary.*

On the occasion of...we...
> - *On the occasion of your company's tenth anniversary, we would like to express our hopes for your continued prosperity.*

Invitations (informal)

Do you want to...?
> - *Do you want to join the trek to Mt. Kilmanjaro?*

How about (verb+ing)...?
> - *How about **joining** my work team?*

I was wondering if you would like to...
> - *I was wondering if you would like to share the contents of the book with us.*

I wonder if you'd like to...
> - *I wonder if you'd like to give us a demonstration of the product.*

There's a/an...[EVENT] on [DAY/DATE]. Would you like to go?
> - *There is a motivational seminar on Sunday morning. Would you like to go?*

Would you like to...
> - *Would you like to come to our office party tomorrow night?*

We're going to...Would you like to come along?
> - *We're going to Ristorante Italiano Buono next Friday. Would you like to come along?*

Invitations (formal)

It is with great pleasure that we invite you to attend our [EVENT]... at [VENUE] on [DATE].

> *- It is with great pleasure that we invite you to attend our President's Lecture at the Tokyo International Forum on January 9, 20XX.*

I would like to invite you to...

> *- I would like to invite you to a golf tournament that is taking place next month.*

If you have time, I'd like to invite you...

> *- If you have time, I'd like to invite you to judge a speech competition.*

We'd be glad to have you join us...

> *- We'd be glad to have you join us at the mayor's ball.*

Would you like to join us for [EVENT] at [TIME] [DAY/DATE]?

> *- Would you like to join us for wine tasting at 7 p.m. tomorrow?*

We would be delighted to have you as our ...

> *-We would be delighted to have you as our guest for a wine tasting session tonight.*

[COMPANY] cordially invites you to attend...[EVENT]...on [DATE]

> *- ZZZ Company cordially invites you to attend our annual Music by the Beach event on August 5, 20XX.*

General Opening Lines — emails / letters (mixed bag)

I am writing to ask about...

> - *I am writing to ask about the coding job you advertised in the Friday, November 21st, 20XX issue of the Hong Kong Herald.*

I saw your advertisement...

> - *I saw your advertisement for a bowling club manager in the Nairobi Times and I would like to be considered for the position.*

I received your name and address from...and would like to...

> - *I received your name and address from The Business Connection and would like to find out if you are interested in collaborating with us in developing a new product.*

General Opening Lines — responding to emails / letters (mixed bag)

Please find enclosed...

> - *Please find enclosed a copy of our latest catalog.*

Thank you for your letter regarding...

> - *Thank you for your letter regarding the Lightning Phone A1.*

Thank you for your letter of [DATE] concerning...

> - *Thank you for your letter of September 8, 20XX, concerning the relocation of your office to Detroit.*

Thank you for your letter of...[DATE], in which you...

> - *Thank you for your letter of January 7, 20XX, in which you asked about our company's latest invention, the XYZ Propeller.*

As stated in your letter/email of [DATE],...

> - *As stated in your letter of June 6, 20XX, you wanted a copy of our latest catalog. We have sent it to you under separate cover.*

In reply to your letter of [DATE],...

> - *In reply to your letter of May 7, 20XX, I would like to assure you that the meeting will take place as previously stated.*

General Closing Lines — emails / letters   (mixed bag)

I would be grateful for your quick attention to this matter.	*I would be most grateful for your quick attention to this matter.*
I look forward to hearing from you shortly.	*I look forward to hearing from you soon.*
I look forward to hearing your response.	*I look forward to seeing you again soon.*
I look forward to your reply.	*I look forward with great interest to hearing from you.*
I trust that you will give this matter the urgent attention it requires.	*We look forward to building a strong business relationship with you.*

Rejection of Application

Thank you very much for your application of [DATE] for the position of...
Unfortunately, we cannot...

> - *Thank you very much for your application of June 5, 20XX for the position of marketing manager. Unfortunately, we cannot offer you the position as it has recently been filled.*

I am sorry, but...

> - *I am sorry, but your qualifications do not meet the minimum requirements for the position.*

Thanks very much for submitting your application for the position of...
Unfortunately, we do not...

> - *Thanks very much for submitting your application for the position of computer programmer. Unfortunately, we do not have any openings at the moment.*

Unit 1
Writing Styles:
the good, the bad, and the ugly

Your ability to communicate well will make more difference to your success in life than any other factor. No matter how much you know or how hard you work, your efforts will go unrecognized unless you can communicate successfully to others.

- Jeanette Wortman Gilsdorf, Writer/Educator (USA)

From fashion styles to writing styles

Over the years, there have been many different kinds of clothes fashion. You don't have to be a fashionista, someone who designs, promotes, or follows the latest fashions, to know that the classic style of fashion differs from the casual just as Harajuku style differs from Punk. And then, there are the traditional garments – the Japanese kimono, the Indonesian sarong, or the flowing robes worn in the Middle East. Each of these has a charm all its own. Writing styles are no different. They are not all the same.

Writing styles

The kind of writing style favored in business today is the plain style. This contrasts with the style made famous by bureaucrats, often involving long words and long-winded sentences.

Bureaucratese: *Reduction of air pollution is a primary objective of the Fukuda regime.*

Plain style: *The Fukuda regime plans to reduce air pollution.*

Journalists write a lot. Pretty soon, they discover that they have to write some of the same stuff over and over again. They begin to use some of the same phrases again and again. These handy phrases, known as clichés because they are overused, make the journalist's job easy, but the writing is hardly fresh.

Here are a few clichés favored by poorly-skilled journalists:

- a storm dumped more than x amount of
- body of a dead man
- highly placed official
- in a surprise move

Journalese:

A reclusive man, with no fixed address, unleashed a litany of insults and an unprovoked attack on a highly placed official. Amid a burgeoning crisis spawned by this event, the body of a dead man, believed to be the official, was found after a storm dumped more than 10 inches of rain on the capital.

This kind of writing will not take you places. On the other hand, consider the plain style of one of the world's richest people, American investor Warren Buffett. The following is taken from Berkshire Hathaway's annual report for 2006:

Charlie Munger – my partner and Berkshire's vice chairman – and I run what has turned out to be a big business, one with 217,000 employees and annual revenues approaching $100 billion. We certainly didn't plan it that way. Charlie began as a lawyer, and I thought of myself as a security analyst. ...I've taken the easy route, just sitting back and working through great managers who run their own shows. My only tasks are to cheer them on, sculpt and harden our corporate culture, and make major capital-allocation decisions. Our managers have returned this trust by working hard and effectively.

Now, which part of Buffett's report did you not understand? He uses contractions (I've taken...), he uses commas, dashes, and an easy-going conversational style.

He uses short sentences, and simple words that are meant to express rather than impress. This makes reading his company's annual report a joy rather than the headache that many other reports are to read.

It is this plain style that you should seek to copy. Don't you want your readers to reach for your writing with the same sense of eagerness that Buffett's readers approach his reports? Of course, many people, including shareholders of Berkshire Hathaway, read Buffett's reports because of their interest in how much money he might have made them, but they must appreciate too, that they can easily understand his reports.

Even though Buffett <u>talks on paper</u> with his shareholders, his ideas are not simplistic; he writes about acquisitions, insurance, manufacturing, service, and retail operations, with the same kind of simple words that guarantee that you will understand his ideas.

Be like Warren Buffett – write in a conversational but respectful tone and your writing will be welcome everywhere. Indeed, ordinary words are best to make your meaning clear.

Instead of......	Write....
Assist	Help
Commence	Begin
Close proximity	Near
Complete	fill out
Endeavor	Try
Forward	Send
Herewith is	Here is
Indicate	Show, Tell

Even if you are not a native speaker of English, you probably know hundreds of simple words. It is natural to continue expanding your vocabulary as a learner of the English language but long, unpronounceable words are not the ones you need in order to write clearly. You need to expand your vocabulary, in part, because you want to understand what others write. Moreover, there are times when your large vocabulary would allow you to choose just the perfect word to express your meaning. Still, keep in mind that there is a lot you can say with the words you already know.

Shades of meaning: Using your Thesaurus

You probably have a <u>nice</u> friend, live in a <u>nice</u> city, make <u>nice</u> meals, and make <u>nice</u> with your colleagues. Words like <u>nice</u>, which we tend to overuse, lose their meaning and power to clearly express what it is we want to say.

If you look up the word "nice" in your thesaurus, you will find many other words that are close in meaning to it. Maybe, one of these other words fits better with the meaning that you have in mind.

If you are not sure about the meanings of the synonyms you find in your thesaurus, use the dictionary.

SYNONYMS (words with the same or similar meaning as another word in the same language)

ANTONYMS (words with opposite meaning to a particular word in the same language)

In the exercise on the next page, first find synonyms to NICE. Choose five of the words that come up. Then, find the exact meaning of each synonym and use the word in a sentence.

UNIT 1: Assignment 1

Write an email to a good friend explaining what you have learned from this unit so far. Encourage your friend to improve his or her writing.

_____

_____

_____

_____

_____

_____

_____

_____

_____

_____

_____

_____

_____

_____

_____

_____

_____

UNIT 1: Assignment 2

You have just heard that an overseas-based colleague of yours, Peter Tamachu, has come to the city/town in which you live and will stay for a week. You are wondering if he will have time to get together for lunch or coffee.

Send him an email to find out if this might be possible. Let him know what might be a good time for you. Keep in mind that Peter is in your city for business.

_____

_____

_____

_____

_____

_____

_____

_____

_____

_____

_____

_____

UNIT 1: Assignment 3

Your company is considering translating a number of documents from one language to another. These would be made available to the company's overseas branches. Find out from Fancy Footwork Translations (Email: fftrans@bizcanada.com) how much it would cost (for 10 pages) along with other details such as turnaround.

_____

_____

_____

_____

_____

_____

_____

_____

_____

_____

_____

_____

_____

_____

_____

Unit 2
IBC: Introduction, Body, Conclusion

In the English language, one of the most common frameworks, whether one is writing an email, a speech, or an essay, is the notion of Introduction, Body, and Conclusion.

The Introduction can do any of the following:

- Present the main idea
- State what you want
- Share some good news
- Share an important fact

The Body might cover any of the following:

- Give reasons
- Provide facts and figures (statistics)
- Ask specific questions
- Explain further
- Comparisons

The Conclusion might include the following:

- Ask for action
- Recap or summarize
- End on a positive note

Here is a sample letter using the IBC framework.

Subject: Sales Team A -- Meeting on July 26th

Introduction: Sales Team A will have a meeting in Room 216 on Friday, July 26th, 2013 starting from 3 p.m.

Body: The purpose of this meeting is to discuss new training options and to review our progress. The meeting will be chaired by Kenji Arudou; the agenda is attached. If you have any questions or concerns before the meeting, please contact me as soon as possible.

Conclusion/ Close   I look forward to seeing you at Friday's meeting.

Regards,
Junko Hayashi

Note: Closings to Avoid for Business Letters

Here are some closings you do not want to use for a business letter. They are okay in nost other situations, but just don't use them to end business letters.

Always
Cheers
Love
Take care

UNIT 2: Assignment 1
Write an email to a good friend explaining what you have learned from this unit so far. Encourage your friend to improve his or her writing.

_____

_____

_____

_____

_____

_____

_____

_____

_____

_____

_____

_____

_____

_____

_____

_____

_____

_____

UNIT 2: Assignment 2

Try as you might, you are unable to finish paperwork before deadlines. You believe your workload is too heavy and that help from others would be a good idea. Send an email to your boss outlining why you could benefit from having an assistant.

_____

_____

_____

_____

_____

_____

_____

_____

_____

_____

_____

_____

_____

UNIT 2: Assignment 3

You think that an employee suggestion box will help improve your company's overall practices, and perhaps, profits. Share the potential benefits of having a suggestion box with your colleagues.

_____

_____

_____

_____

_____

_____

_____

_____

_____

_____

_____

_____

_____

_____

_____

Unit 3
Prepare, Write, Edit (PWE)

Prepare

If you want to write well, sometimes, you have to slow down. Before you write, take time to think. Take time to prepare. This means considering why you need to write, who you are writing to or for, what information you need, and even what tone you should use.

Preparation: Simple or complex?

Preparing may be simple if all you are doing is writing a letter to a friend to give information about an upcoming event. On the other hand, planning can take more thought and time if you have to describe the full range of your company's activities. There is a world of difference in how much preparation is required in the two situations. Preparation may be as simple as making a phone call to a colleague to confirm who is responsible for dealing with a particular matter. Or, it might be as involved as having to search through specialized databases to get some key information.

Purpose

Before you start writing, know your purpose. Are you trying to answer a question or are you trying to persuade someone? Having a clear purpose can save you time.

Know Your Reader

Knowing your reader is also important. How you write to your friend who is vacationing in Switzerland is likely to be different from how you write to the head of a big conglomerate that is considering becoming your client. The tone will differ. For example, if you are writing to the president of a big company, you might want to use a slightly more formal approach. On the other hand, if you are writing to someone and you know that the person prefers a friendly approach, it would not do to write a letter that is so formal.

Before you write, consider the following:

1. What's your reader's background?
2. What does the reader know already?
3. What does the reader need to know?
4. What are the reader's interests and values?

If you are writing to someone that you have never had any contact with, it is going to be difficult to know the answers to these questions. In that case, use your knowledge of the world and your imagination to create an image of the reader.

In any case, in order to have your letter taken seriously in business, it has to look and sound professional.

Your Image

Pay attention to the kind of image you want to project. People who read your letters, memos, or reports will make judgments about you based on how you present yourself on paper or in other forms of correspondence such as email.

Image is important because, depending on your tone, your formatting, and even your grammar, you may come across as careless, thoughtful or inconsiderate.

Some might even read a letter or a note and decide that the writer is insincere. Your choice of words, what you say and how you say it, all contribute towards creating an image of you in the reader's mind. What kind of image do you want that to be?

Organize

Organizing your writing can be useful to the reader. It can also be useful to you as a writer because it forces you to think more clearly about how one idea connects with another. We cover reports later on, but you may have noticed that many reports are broken down into major headings, and sometimes, subheadings.

Outline

A simple outline can be a list of points and sometimes, subpoints. Think also about the order in which to present the material.

Pay attention to organization, logic, and order.

Email — Subject Headings

Do you pay attention to your email subject headings? If you do, you can help both yourself and the recipient. Writing a subject heading that is meaningful can help the recipient to decide how important the message is and make it easy to retrieve when necessary. A simple "Hello" in the subject line is harmless enough but it is not of much use to a busy person who is trying to figure out how to prioritize responses to dozens, if not hundreds, of emails.

Let your subject lines be short, meaningful, and free of filler words.

Here are some examples:
- Requesting input on social media strategy
- Potential collaboration on container housing
- Sales Managers: Quarterly Meeting this Friday

In all the email assignments in this text, be sure to include a subject heading.

Sorry, wrong question!

Someone might write to ask you about something but because of your greater knowledge of the issue, you realize that the person is asking the wrong question. In such a case, it would be proper to share with the person why you think another question might have been better.

You may answer the writer's original question and then show why another question might have been better.

Rough draft

Writing an email, a letter, or a report, is not always easy. Even some professional writers do get stuck — sometimes for days! This is the famous (or infamous) "writer's block." Rather than staring forever at the blank sheet or screen and waiting for the perfect sentence to come floating in, why not just start even if the words don't seem to come out right? In fact, what you write at first does not have to be perfect. Think, plan, and write. Then, worry later about how to shape or reshape the piece. This is how some of the best communicators work. They do not seek perfection in their first attempts. In that sense, the process of writing can become an effective thinking tool. Your first draft may lead to a second or even a third attempt before you're satisfied with the tenor of your message.

I write because I don't know what I think until I read what I say.

- Flannery O'Connnor, American writer

Editing

The newspaper articles and letters and books we read often seem perfect. In truth, some of the most respected authors, including Ernest Hemingway and James Michener, freely admitted to spending enormous amounts of time editing their works and even having others go over their work both for substance and style. Even for a short letter, consider going over it. You may find a typo here, a word that does not fit there, or still more, a sentence that could be shortened without losing the key point.

Editing can involve more than just checking for grammar. It can involve cutting out words or phrases or even an entire paragraph. It can involve rewriting parts of the piece or rearranging or reorganizing the order of the ideas you seek to present.

Weaknesses

It helps to be aware of your own weaknesses so that you can pay attention to those areas during the writing process. Are you weak in spelling? Is your grammar a little rusty? If you know where your weaknesses lie, you can ensure that those weaknesses do not become a major handicap in your writing.

UNIT 3: Assignment 1

Your company is holding a workshop and lecture series on Saturday, November 7, 20XX. You need a lectern but you are unable to buy or rent one. One of your affiliate companies, which is two blocks away from your office, has a lectern that you want to borrow. The General Manager is Ms Kirsten Kardalian. Send an email requesting the use of the lectern; mention when you would like to pick it up and when you would return it.

_____

_____

_____

_____

_____

_____

_____

_____

_____

_____

_____

_____

UNIT 3: Assignment 2

You have recently discovered MOOCs – massive open online courses – which offer courses in a wide variety of fields. You think your colleagues would greatly benefit from these learning opportunities. Send an email to all your colleagues informing them about these opportunities.

_____

_____

_____

_____

_____

_____

_____

_____

_____

_____

_____

_____

_____

_____

_____

_____

UNIT 3: Assignment 3

You met someone called Letitia Azuma at an industry conference; you think you could be of mutual help to each other professionally. Send her an email expressing how happy you are to have met her. Share your hopes for this professional relationship.

_____

_____

_____

_____

_____

_____

_____

_____

_____

_____

_____

_____

_____

_____

Unit 4
Focus on Numbers

Quite frequently, in our communications, we do not only have to share opinions and proposals, but also, we might have to report on statistics, money, and time. So, we cannot ignore numbers.

Ordinal Numbers: Attention!

It's always disappointing to see someone write 2rd or 3th or 9st. Maybe, people make such errors because they do not know how ordinal numbers, which show the position of something in a series, are constructed. Here is a review:

First	1st	Sixteenth	16th
Second	2nd	Seventeenth	17th
Third	3rd	Eighteenth	18th
Fourth	4th	Nineteenth	19th
Fifth	5th	Twentieth	20th
Sixth	6th	Twenty-first	21st
Seventh	7th	Twenty-second	22nd
Eighth	8th	Twenty-third	23rd
Ninth	9th	Twenty-fourth	24th
Tenth	10th	Twenty-fifth	25th
Eleventh	11th	Twenty-sixth	26th
Twelfth	12th	Twenty-seventh	27th
Thirteenth	13th	Twenty-eighth	28th
Fourteenth	14th	Twenty-ninth	29th
Fifteenth	15th	Thirtieth	30th

So, if you want to make an appointment, make sure that you abbreviate the date correctly:

Let's meet on the July 1st.

Let's get together on February 23rd.

It would be a pleasure to see you on November 2nd.

Cardinal Numbers and Dates

When you are writing dates, use cardinal numbers (1, 2, 3, 4, 5, 6, 7, 8, etc.) rather than ordinal numbers (1st, 2nd, 3rd, 4th, 5th, 6th, 7th, 8th, etc.).

For example,

We shall hold the workshop on November 16, 20XX.

*On February 8, 20XX, we shall hold an orientation session
for new employees.*

Here are some additional points to keep in mind when dealing with numbers. Some "experts" suggest that when you are writing a document and you mention numbers between one and ten, they should be in words. Others say that this should extend to ninety-nine. Since the experts cannot agree, maybe, you would have to make your own decision as to which of these two seems proper to you.

Zero to Ten (Words)
Above Ten (Numerals/Figures)

Zero to Ninety-nine (Words)
100 and above (Figures/Numerals)

Number at beginning of sentence (Words)

It is also recommended that you not use numbers at the beginning of a sentence.

Instead of writing

2001 was a good year for stocks in America

write

The year 2000 was a good one for stocks in America.

Cluster of numbers (Figures)

When you have a bunch of numbers together, it is better to present them in figures rather than words.

The jersey numbers of the players on the basketball court included the following: 7, 9, 17, 23, and 99.

U.S. Style (Also used in the U.K. and Mexico)

In the U.S. style of presenting numbers, note the use of the commas to break up the digits.

1,765,000

International System of Metric Measurement (space separations)

On the other hand, spacing is used to do the separation in the international system, as follows:

1 765 000

Dates

American style

> February 23, 2010
>
> September 30, 2011

> British Style
>
> 7 April, 1999
>
> 19 October, 2007

Time

> 6:15 a.m.
>
> 8 p.m.

or

> five o'clock in the evening
>
> 12 noon
>
> 12 midnight
>
> three o'clock in the morning

Measurements

When you are presenting measurements of any kind, such as the length and breadth of a table, the area of a room, the height of a building, it is recommended that you do so in actual numbers. They stand out better for the reader. For example,

> 3.7 meters clearance
>
> 20,715 people
>
> 7 months
>
> 5-inch nails

> Temperature (- 50° C)
>
> Even small numbers (1%)

Money

Here below are some of the most common ways money is presented. In this example, U.S. dollars are used, but the same could apply to other currencies that are being presented in English language correspondence.

$5 $15 $150 $150,000

$15 million

$15 billion

$15.5 billion

$7.08

$19.99

Ratios

7:1:5

5:1

10:1

UNIT 4: Assignment 1

Your company has hired a new head for the IT department. You are busy, so you will not be able to meet him for a while. Send an email welcoming this new hire, Mr Mitara Lokko, to your company. You want Mr Lokko to know who you are and perhaps how you might work together in the future.

_____

_____

_____

_____

_____

_____

_____

_____

_____

_____

_____

_____

_____

_____

UNIT 4: Assignment 2

You have been working with a printing company for the last 18 months, but they are always late with your work and there have been times when their mistakes have delayed your projects. You want to end your company's relationship with them.

Send an email to the Head of Operations, Ms Jana Smithson, explaining your decision.

_____

_____

_____

_____

_____

_____

_____

_____

_____

_____

_____

UNIT 4: Assignment 3

You have been asked by the head of research in your company, Ms. Itsuko Kameyama, to itemize things you have on your desk, including pens, pencils, erasers, computers, ink stands, etc. She also wants to know if you are willing to take part in a one-on-one interview about ergonomics. Indicate in your reply, along with the number of different items you have on your desk, whether you will be available for the interview and what might be a good time for y

_____

_____

_____

_____

_____

_____

_____

_____

_____

_____

_____

_____

Unit 5
Grammar: Front and Center

Below are some common grammatical errors: sentence fragments, run-on sentences, and the comma splice. A review of this section will help you eliminate these kinds of mistakes. Meanwhile, continue to be a diligent student of grammar.

Sentence Fragments

A sentence fragment is a group of words that is presented as a sentence but falls short of the label because it lacks one or more key ingredients of a sentence. An actual sentence, according to the Merriam Webster dictionary is "a group of words that makes a statement, asks a question, or expresses a command, wish or exclamation."

The word 'fragment' refers to "a part" and is thus incomplete.
Here is an example:

Not gone.

The above is an example of a sentence fragment. What is not gone? The two words could be a part (a fragment) of a sentence but by themselves they do not make much sense.

In fairness, novelists and newspaper article writers sometimes use sentence fragments to achieve certain effects. Such writers are aware of when and why they should not use fragments. When they choose to use fragments, they may have a good reason to do so. If you study grammar well enough, you may also decide that in some of your writings you will include a fragment. As long as you know what you are doing, that is all right.

Consider also, that, while sentence fragments may be all right in a novel, in the business world, you do not want to appear too casual to the point of being perceived as careless. So in business, you might want to avoid using sentence fragments.

Run-on sentences

With a run-on sentence, two or more independent clauses are joined but without the correct punctuation. For example,

We are going to the pool we shall eat hamburger there.

In the above there are two sentences, not one.

When you have a sentence that lacks the correct break such as a comma, semicolon, or period, you have a run-on sentence.

With the proper punctuation, the problem of run-on is easily solved.

We are going to the pool, and we shall eat hamburger there.
We are going to the pool; we shall eat hamburger there.

Sometimes the run-on sentence may come about not because your grammar is poor but because you were in a hurry and simply missed putting in the proper punctuation mark.

Review your writing.

The Comma Splice

When two independent clauses are separated by a comma instead of a period or a semi-colon, this is called a comma splice. This is sometimes deliberately used by novel writers, but some people frown upon such usage.

Here are some examples of the comma splice:
    a) *The wolf stood in the garden, the cat stayed in the tree.*

In the above, the two parts are better separated by a period or a semicolon. Instead, they are separated by a comma.

    b) *The company makes electronic gadgets, the company also makes beauty products.*

Here are some possibilities for fixing the above:

a)   *The wolf stood in the garden, and the cat stayed in the tree.*
      The wolf stood in the garden; the cat stayed in the tree.
      The wolf stood in the garden. The cat stayed in the tree.

b)   *The company makes electronic gadgets; the company also makes beauty products.*

      The company makes electronic gadgets, and it also makes beauty products.

      The company makes electronic gadgets. The company also makes beauty products.

      The company makes electronic gadgets. It also makes beauty products.

Parallel structure

Above, you see two lines that are parallel to each other. The lines extend in the same direction. In graphic arts and in mathematics, such parallel lines are considered pleasing to the eye. In both writing and speaking, we can use parallelism to add a bit of flavor to what may otherwise be boring writing.

I want a cat. I want a dog. I enjoy swimming in the pool.

In the above, the first two sentences are parallel while the pattern of the third is different.

I enjoy eating sushi. I enjoy drinking juice. I enjoy dancing salsa.

This works better as the three sentences follow the same pattern.

Many notable writers and speakers have used parallelism to good effect, including Canadian writer Margaret Atwood and United States presidents Abraham Lincoln and Barack Obama. It is not only in the field of politics where you can spice up your language with parallelism. You can use parallelism in your letters, memos, incident reports, and other correspondence.

Examples:

We are going to dig the ditches, install the piling, and build the structure.

Some stood, others sat; some cheered, others cried.

We shall hire creative people, design great products, and provide terrific service to our customers.

Conciseness

Why use a hundred words to say something when you can say the same thing in twenty? Being concise means using only a few appropriate words to express your meaning.

Semicolon

The semicolon poses a problem for many writers. Consider this: You have two sentences (actually independent clauses). Each of them can stand on its own but there is a relationship between the two. In such a case, you can use a semicolon to separate them. For example:

My friend has two pets. One is a dog; the other is a cat.
She is Roman Catholic; he is Protestant.
The top floor office is huge; the ground floor office is small.

Quotation marks

When you cite someone else's words in writing, it is standard practice to put those words in quotation marks. This is a signal that the words are not your own. Here's an example:

The principal said, "You must come to school on time tomorrow. I will have something very special for you all."

Paraphrase

If you borrow ideas from someone and you change the words of the original work, that kind of treatment does not use quotation marks. Likewise, when you report what someone else said in your own words, you do not need to use quotation marks. In such cases, you just mention the name or title of the writer or speaker as having been the source of the idea.

The principal told us to go to school on time the following day and that she would have something very special for us all.

Apostrophe

We generally use the apostrophe to show possession, that something belongs to someone or something.

The dog's breakfast.

The teacher's pet.

When it comes to the third person singular (it), however, we write:

*The dog wagged **its** tail.* <= [Note that there is no apostrophe]
*The dog wagged **it's** tail.* = [The dog wagged **it is** tail] <= this does not make sense

***It's** hot in here.* [This is a contraction of 'It is" — in this case, the use of the apostrophe is correct.]

Verbs

Whenever possible, use verbs. They strengthen your writing.

Instead of...	Write...
Sakamoto is the winner of last week's marathon.	Sakamoto **won** last week's marathon.
There are so many cherry trees in Japan.	Japan **abounds** in cherry trees.

Hyphen

When we use two or more words as a unit to modify a noun or pronoun, we hyphenate the two-word unit. In this case **two-word** is a modifying unit. Here are a few examples:

one-way road / **fresh-faced** youth / **eager-eyed** soldier / **two-tier** system

Spelling

In this age of spell-check on every computer, we should not be making too many spelling errors. Take time to go over your work and correct any errors.

Also, don't forget that the spell-check function cannot pick up words that are spelled correctly but do not fit the meaning you had in mind.

If you are not sure about a word, check the meaning to be sure that you are using the correct one. It is not uncommon to find reputable organizations writing **principle**, for example, instead of **principal** or vice versa.

Use Active Sentences

In an active sentence, the subject does the action of the verb.

The sales director visited all the local branches.

The passive sentence does not focus on the doer of an action.

All the plants in the lobby were watered.

Use active sentences as much as possible. You might find occasion to use passive sentences, but the active sentence is much more forceful.

UNIT 5: Assignment 1

You made an inexcusable mistake at work for which you have apologized in person to your colleagues. You feel, however, that an email apology as a follow-up will allow you to express more fully the sincerity of your apology. Send an email to your colleagues affirming your regret for the unintended error and assuring them that such a mistake shall never occur again.

UNIT 5: Assignment 2

Your company has purchased some equipment from a foreign company and wired 6 million yen in payment. Write an email to the company informing them of when you sent the funds and asking for them to confirm receipt as well as tell you when you will receive their products.

_____

_____

_____

_____

_____

_____

_____

_____

_____

_____

_____

_____

_____

_____

_____

UNIT 5: Assignment 3

Dear Sir/Madam:

We are considering using your company's services. Please let us know what makes your company different from your competitors.

Sincerely,
Rhonda Rowad

_____

_____

_____

_____

_____

_____

_____

_____

_____

_____

_____

_____

_____

Unit 6
YOU and ME

You probably work hard. You probably want whatever advantage you can get in life. You probably do not mind retiring early or taking a couple of vacations every year. Your life is important to you and you probably think a lot about how to make your life sweeter, better, more comfortable, and less stressful.

When you are writing letters or emails, please keep in mind that just as you worry about things that affect your life, others may similarly worry about the things that touch their own lives.

If you are writing to others in the hope of getting their cooperation, it would be a mistake to focus only on your needs. People are more likely to respond well to you if they know that you care about them and their needs or concerns.

A "YOU" oriented approach, therefore, will win you more friends and help you better influence business associates than an "I, ME, MY, or MINE" centered approach. Read the following two letters and determine which is more likely to get the desired results.

SAMPLE LETTER A:

Dear Dr Mococan:

My name is Tomohiro Ogawa and I work for a pharmaceutical company in Tokyo, Japan. I have made some incredible advances in the field of influenza research and I am often told that I am destined for greatness, and that I might even win the Nobel Prize in the near future. Honestly speaking, I don't pay much attention to that.

Anyway, I am interested in learning more about the technique you pioneered, the Mococan Influenza Assay. I am working on a paper now that will be presented at a conference in Linz, Austria, in the coming year. I need to talk about your method briefly but I confess that I am not as clear about the details as I should. As such, any materials you can send me, including articles you have written, chapters of books, pamphlets, or personal notes, etc., would be greatly appreciated.

I look forward to hearing from you soon.

Yours truly,

Tomohiro Ogawa

SAMPLE LETTER B:

Dear Dr Mococan:

I note with great interest your many superb contributions to the field of pharmaceutical research in general and influenza research in particular.

One of the techniques you pioneered, the Mococan Influenza Assay, is of great interest to my company. We understand, however, that it is proprietary; we would, therefore, like to seek your permission to apply the methodology in our research. As such, if there are any conditions attached to the use of the Mococan Influenza Assay, kindly inform us at your earliest possible convenience.

Your leadership in the field of pharmaceutical research is a great inspiration to me and the other members of my team.

We look forward with great interest to hearing from you.

Sincerely,

Tomohiro Ogawa

COMMENTS ON THE TWO LETTERS

What did you like or dislike about each of the two letters?

Which has a better likelihood of getting the desired results?

To write for results:

- Think "YOU"
- Avoid too much "I, Me, My, or Mine"

- Offer sincere compliments
- Show that you know something about the recipient (something positive, that is)

- Be considerate of the other person's time
- Use respectful language

- Avoid showing off
- Avoid wasting the reader's time with irrelevant points

UNIT 6: Assignment 1
You have just received an email from an old friend. He writes:

Hey buddy,

What's up? You're doing all right, I hope. I'm kinda struggling in my new job. You see, my boss has been giving me all kinds of writing assignments. I have heard that you are taking a business writing course. Send me some tips ASAP on how I can improve my writing.

Cheers,
Peter Lamkin (Your Old Friend — Still Young!)

_____

_____

_____

_____

_____

_____

_____

_____

_____

_____

_____

UNIT 6: Assignment 2

Ms Zana Lattimer has worked in your office for five years. She is leaving in the next two weeks, both because of family issues and the need to explore new professional horizons abroad. She is an exceptionally good employee and you want to express your sadness at her impending departure and to wish her well in her future endeavors.

_____

_____

_____

_____

_____

_____

_____

_____

_____

_____

_____

_____

UNIT 6: Assignment 3

A colleague from another country is coming to work with you. She is not sure exactly what your job entails and wants you to send a brief description of what you do.

_____

_____

_____

_____

_____

_____

_____

_____

_____

_____

_____

_____

_____

Unit 7
IDAC : Your 4-point Plan

British writing consultant Shirley Taylor, suggests a 4-point plan for writing that can work as well for letters as for emails: IDAC.

IDAC[2]

I	INTRODUCTION	Give your reason for writing Refer to the letter you are about to reply to
D	DETAILS	Give information and ask for all relevant information
A	ACTION	Mention expected response date Mention when you want to meet
C	CLOSE	Sign off

Use of IDAC

For most emails and letters, it is possible to use the four-step formula (IDAC) to either write or respond. IDAC begins with an **Introduction**, which tries to capture the main point you want to make. Then follows **Details**, in which you present in-depth information on the subject. The **Action** part is for decisions such as meeting the person you are corresponding with, asking for a follow-up phone call or email, or in fact, anything that requires action on your part, on the part of the addressee, or on someone else's part. Finally, there is the **Close**, which you should keep simple.

---

2 Shirley Taylor, *Model Business Letters, E-mails, and Other Business Letters,* Pearson, UK, 2012.

Here's an example:

	Dear Ms Yvonne Motozuki:
Introduction	We have received your request for a new credit card for your seven-year-old son.
Details	Newly-released policy guidelines from our headquarters prohibit us from issuing credit cards to children under the age of twelve. Even though you have been a longstanding client, we are, unfortunately, unable to fulfill this request.
Action	You may want to apply for the Junior Debit Card, which was issued early this year, and has become popular with parents who want to teach their children financial responsibility. If you are interested, please give me a call anytime on weekdays between 9 a.m. and 12 noon.
Closing	I look forward to hearing from you. Sincerely, Peter Samarama Special Customer Accounts

Sample Apology Letter

Dear Ms Leila Sayuri:

I: I would like to apologize for the delay in dispatching the 35 replacement wheel covers that you ordered on November 2, 20XX.

D: We have ordered them and our tracking system shows that there was an error in the shipper's data, which has caused the delay.

A: Ms Sayuri, be assured that you will receive the hubcaps, No. 345, by Friday, December 7, 20XX.

C: Kindly accept our apologies for any inconvenience caused.

Sincerely,

Kenichi Ogasawara
Senior Logistics Manager

IDAC – Just a Guideline, not a Commandment

As useful as IDAC is, there may be times when you find that you can present your message without covering all the elements of IDAC. Maybe, you will find need at some point to combine the details and the action or combine the introduction and the details.

In the following sample collection letters, does the writer observe IDAC?

Sample Collection Letters

REMINDER 1

November 16, 20XX

Dear Ms Janet Machado,

We hope that the 1000 20XX Acura model MDX K & N Air Filters (Gauze) that we shipped to you were all satisfactory.

You agreed to make payment by November 15, 20XX; this is a reminder in case there was an oversight.

Please disregard this message if you have transferred the funds into our account.

Sincerely,

Majime Ohara
Accounts Manager

REMINDER 2

December 16, 20XX

Dear Ms Janet Machado,

Please note that we have still not received payment for the 1000 20XX Acura model MDX K & N Air Filters (Gauze) that we shipped to you in October 20XX.

You agreed to make payment by November 15, 20XX.

Enclosed is our account information.

If by chance, you have already paid, please disregard this letter and accept our apologies.

Sincerely,

Majime Ohara
Accounts Manager

REMINDER 3

January 16, 20XX

Dear Ms Janet Machado,

Our records show that payment for the 1000 20XX Acura model MDX K & N Air Filters (Gauze) that we shipped to you in October 20XX is over 60 days past the agreed-upon payment date.

Our policy requires that we refer you to a collection agency, which we are reluctant to do.

Please pay within the next 10 days otherwise we will have no choice but to refer your account for collections.

We trust that you will attend to this matter with the utmost urgency.

Sincerely,

Majime Ohara
Accounts Manager

SAMPLE ESTIMATE LETTER

Dear Mr Rowan Atkingan:

Please find enclosed the estimate you recently requested on XXXX parts.

Product	Number	Quantity	Price	Quantity X Price
XXXX				

This quote is valid until December 15, 20XX.

If you have any questions please contact us, and we will respond without delay.

Sincerely,

Junko Nishi
Sales Executive

UNIT 7: Assignment 1

A senior executive, Ms Shivangi Harper, is going to take over the leadership of your section and wants you to send her an email describing a project you are working on now or one that you worked on in the past.

_____

_____

_____

_____

_____

_____

_____

_____

_____

_____

_____

_____

_____

_____

_____

UNIT 7: Assignment 2

Mr Kojo Sweeney helped you prepare some PowerPoint slides. Send a brief email of thanks to him. Be sure to mention that you will need his help again in the near future. Also, give him the assurance that you will be taking steps to learn the program so that you do not have to depend on him forever.

_____

_____

_____

_____

_____

_____

_____

_____

_____

_____

_____

_____

UNIT 7: Assignment 3

You have just mailed a package of your company's services to Ms Lanelle Fox. It will take two days to arrive.

Send her an email to let her know about the package you sent. Also, give her your contact information in case she has any questions that she needs answered.

_____

_____

_____

_____

_____

_____

_____

_____

_____

_____

_____

_____

Unit 8
IDAC: I is for Introduction

It is not always easy to grab a reader's attention and hold it. In writing an email or a letter, your first sentence, your **Introduction** is very important. Some people, however, find it difficult to write a good introduction.

The following technique will help you to write good introductions when writing a letter or email.

I Want To Inform You That...(For Letters Or Emails)

Using the above expression, you can capture the main point that you want to convey. To do so, start your draft letter with the following words, "I want to tell you that...." or "I want to inform you that..."

Here are some examples:

- *I want to inform you that the president will be visiting your office on Friday, December 5th, 20XX.*

- *I want to inform you that the Yatota Ping Pong team won the 21st annual sports competition in Oslo this year.*

- *I want to inform you that you are invited to a party at 451 Sabran Lane, Sussex.*

Once you are sure that the first line captures what you truly want to say, you may cancel the first part, i.e., "I want to tell you that" or "I want to inform you that..."

For example,

> ~~I want to inform you that~~ *The president will be visiting your office on Friday, December 5th, 20xx.*

> ~~I want to inform you that~~ *The Yatota Ping Pong team won the 21st annual sports competition in Oslo this year.*

> ~~I want to inform you that~~ *You are invited to a party at 451 Sabran Lane, Sussex.*

Short Paragraphs are All Right

Businesspeople are busy people. Get straight to the point at the beginning of your email or letter. You do not have to write long-winded paragraphs and bury the most important thing you want to say.

Short paragraphs make your writing more inviting to read. Note that it is even possible to have a one-line paragraph.

UNIT 8: Assignment 1

Exercise: I want to tell you that...

Using the phrase "I want to tell you that..." as a starting point, try to create a sentence that could serve as an introduction to a letter or email.

Example: New website design

> ** ~~I want to tell you that~~...Our company's website will be redesigned in the coming weeks.*

> ** Our company's website will be redesigned in the coming weeks.*

1. Urgent meeting: _____

_____

_____

2. New IT staff member: _____

_____

_____

3. Earthquake drill: _____

_____

_____

4. New food delivery service: _____

_____

_____

5. Year-end party: _____

_____

_____

6. Teleconference meeting: _____

_____

_____

7. Invitation of colleagues to a routine meeting: _____

_____

_____

8. Request to borrow an item from a colleague: _____

_____

_____

9. Inquiry about a negotiation seminar to be held next month: _____

_____

_____

10. A complaint: _____

_____

_____

UNIT 8: Assignment 2

Your supervisor says: "We need a new fax machine. Send an email to KokuFax Incorporated (info@kokufax.jp) and ask them to send us a copy of their latest catalog. Also, find out if they can send a salesperson to our office some time next week."

_____

_____

_____

_____

_____

_____

_____

_____

_____

_____

_____

_____

_____

UNIT 8: Assignment 3

You had been negotiating with a company, Bambers Trust, over the last five months to sell them some products. You've come to an agreement on both price and terms. This morning, you got an email from the head of the company asking for 5% more reduction on the price you had agreed upon. You really want to do business with this company. At the same time, a 5% reduction will hurt your business badly. Send an email to Ms Zellenika Omamu, CEO, of Bambers Trust.

_____

_____

_____

_____

_____

_____

_____

_____

_____

_____

_____

_____

_____

_____

Unit 9
Common Errors in Business Writing

The same mistakes often come up again and again in business writing. This is good news. It means that if you are able to overcome these errors, you could improve your writing considerably.

Here are a few of them:

• Too many words (save your reader time by getting to the point)
• Use of jargon, technical words, and unfamiliar acronyms (if the reader doesn't understand the word or term, you have not properly shared your message)
• Lack of organization (use an outline/have a plan before you begin)

Get Editing Help

It is difficult for some writers to check their own work. But every writer ought to make the effort. You may also get someone to check your writing, especially if it is a long report. If it is a short report or letter, sometimes, all you need to do is put it aside for a while and get back to it later. When you return to the work with a pair of fresh eyes you often see things that you could not see before.

Mind your tone

Often, how we say something is just as important as what we say. Sometimes, long after people have forgotten what we said, they might still remember how what we said affected them. Human beings are creatures of emotion. This includes businesspeople! So, it is important to consider your tone. It is, perhaps, with this in mind that American poet Maya Angelou wrote,

I've learned that people will forget what you said, people will forget what you did, but people will never forget how you made them feel.

If you do not craft your message carefully, it is possible for the reader to feel disrespected or even attacked. Please mind your tone.

Logical flow

Making use of a brief outline can be very useful. It can be as simple as a point-by-point list of the topics you want to cover. Make sure that the points follow a logical order up to the conclusion. Once you have the points down, think hard about how you can seize the reader's attention.

If you do not grab the reader in the first few seconds, you cannot guarantee that he or she will read on till the end.

Welcome plain language

For decades, English speakers maintained a somewhat rigid separation between the spoken language and the written language. Written English often involved multisyllabic words and long sentences. Readers sometimes had to go look for their dusty dictionaries to find out what the writer was trying to say. Spoken language, however, has often been more direct. Remember the advice, "Write like you talk?" If you write as though you were talking directly to the reader, you can't go wrong.

Say no to clichés

Clichés are overused phrases. When such phrases first came into fashion, they may have seemed fresh, but after being used over and over again, they no longer seem fresh. You are better off creating your own fresh-sounding expressions than relying on clichés to carry your writing along.

Here's a sampling of clichés: *ace in the hole; airing dirty laundry; ace up your sleeve; back to square one; acid test; all in a day's work; all hat, no cattle; death and destruction; back against the wall*

UNIT 9: Assignment 1

A customer was put on hold for twenty minutes and forgotten. She has threatened to stop doing business with your company. Write an apology letter to her. She is Ms Yvette Fernando.

_____

_____

_____

_____

_____

_____

_____

_____

_____

_____

_____

_____

_____

UNIT 9: Assignment 2

Your company has a bright idea to get employees to work only four days a week by stretching the workday from 8 am to 8 pm, with a one-hour break between 12 noon and 1 pm. You are not thrilled about the idea and want to discourage the company from carrying it out. Write to the president, Ms Youngsan Park, about your concerns.

UNIT 9: Assignment 3

Your boss says, "We have a number of high school students coming here tomorrow for Career Day exercises. I would like you to give them a five-minute presentation about what you like about working in this company. Send me an email explaining some of the points you intend to make in the presentation." Send to Ms Chen Ronjin.

_____

_____

_____

_____

_____

_____

_____

_____

_____

_____

_____

_____

_____

_____

Unit 10
The Reader's Need: Revisited

The reader is king, queen, prince, or princess – take your pick. If you want to write letters that get quick replies and results, keep your reader forever in mind. Don't keep the attention on you; shine the spotlight on the reader.

Keeping your reader in mind means, first of all, using words that the reader will understand. If you are using words and expressions that require the reader to pick up the dictionary every few words, you might lose the attention you seek. If you are using too many "me's" and "I's" — beware. Rather, let "you" (that is, the reader) be the center of attention.

Analyze the reader

Analyze your reader. Think about your reader's possible needs. If you are aware of the level of knowledge of your client or potential reader, you are more likely to adopt the correct tone and send just the right amount of information that the reader needs. Can you put yourself in the reader's position?

No benefit of eye contact!

When you send an email, you do not have the benefit of eye contact, gestures, or other face-to-face communication signals with the reader. Your writing, therefore, ought to be able to stand on its own! Make sure that what you have written will hold the reader's attention till the end. Otherwise, the letter, memo, or report will be put aside, and promptly forgotten.

Call for action

Let the reader know how you want him or her to respond. Do you want the reader to telephone you? Wire funds? Buy your product?

Readers do not have to guess what you want them to do. So, be explicit. Be clear in making the request, though politely.

UNIT 10: Assignment 1

You have been invited by a client, Ms Melanie Biluyu, to attend a party. You have an important task to complete at work, so you cannot attend. Send Ms Biluyu a brief message explaining that you cannot attend this time.

_____

_____

_____

_____

_____

_____

_____

_____

_____

_____

_____

_____

_____

UNIT 10: Assignment 2

Your colleague has won your company's "Employee of the Year" award. All along, you thought you would win. You are very disappointed. Send an email to congratulate your colleague.

_____

_____

_____

_____

_____

_____

_____

_____

_____

_____

_____

_____

_____

_____

Assignment 3
Your department's photocopier has broken down several times in the last few weeks. You believe that the machine will die soon and that it's probably a good idea to get a replacement. Send an email to Ms Miri Hirano, Section Head.

_____

_____

_____

_____

_____

_____

_____

_____

_____

_____

_____

_____

_____

_____

Unit 11
Know Your Formats

There are many different kinds of formats for written communication. A memo is not a letter and a fax is not an email. Each has its own special format. Being aware of such formats can help you reach your reader in a medium that is both familiar and appropriate.

Common Letter Formats:

- Full Block
- Semi-block/Modified Block

There are many formats for letters but the two mentioned above are the most commonly used. Decide on one style and stick with it. It will make your life easier. In some cases, the company you work for may have decided on a style – a preferred house style – so all you have to do is confirm which one it is and stick with it.

Full Block Style

Ms Johnetta Bigsby[3]	<==	*{Sender's name}*
Write Right International Consultants	<==	*{Name of sender's company}*
17 Lodestar Avenue	<==	*{Sender's address}*
Port Angeles, WA		
98620 USA		
Tel: (360) 555-6666	<==	*{Sender's telephone number}*
December 7, 20XX	<==	*{Date letter written}*
Mr Willy Bakuroyokoyama	<==	*{Recipient's name}*
Bakubaku Shoji Ltd.	<==	*{Name of recipient's company}*
7-7-1 Higashi Shinjuku	<==	*{Recipient's address}*
Shinjuku-ku, Tokyo		
150-9876		

Dear Mr Willy Bakuroyokoyama: *{Note use of colon in salutation/*
                                                           comma also OK}

SUBJECT: Full Block

Your desire to choose a house style for your letters is an admirable one.

We highly recommend the Full Block style because it is easy to use. Everything starts from the left, whether it's the recipient's address, date, salutation or complimentary close. Of course, if you are using a letterhead then you do not have to write down the address of the sender (yours), as this would already be shown on the letterhead.

Following the complimentary close, be sure to include your name and leave ample space, about four lines, for your signature. You may also include your title.

Sincerely,

Johnetta Bigsby
Writing Consultant

---

3 Sender's name here may be omitted

Modified Block Style

{Sender's name}	==>	Ms Johnetta Bigsby[4]
{Name of sender's company}		Write Right International Consultants
{Sender's address}		17 Lodestar Avenue
		Port Angeles, WA
		98620 USA
{Sender's telephone number} ==>		Tel: (360) 555-6666
{Date letter written}	==>	December 7, 20XX

Mr Willy Bakuroyokoyama	<==	*{Recipient's name}*
Bakubaku Shoji Ltd.	<==	*{Name of recipient's company}*
7-7-1 Higashi Shinjuku	<==	*{Recipient's address}*
Shinjuku-ku, Tokyo		
150-9876		

Dear Mr Willy Bakuroyokoyama:	<==	*{Note use of colon in salutation/ comma also OK}*

SUBJECT: Modified block style

Your desire to choose a house style for your letters is a good idea.

An option you might want to consider is the Modified Block Style. In this case, the sender's name, address, and date, as well as the complimentary close and signature block, are indented towards the right. Everything else stays on the left.

Following the complimentary close, be sure to include your name and leave ample space, about four lines, for your signature. You may also include your title.

{Complimentary Close}   Sincerely,

{Job title}   Johnetta Bigsby
Writing Consultant

---

4 Sender's name here may be omitted

UNIT 11: **Assignment 1**

You have received a questionnaire from A2Z Seminars and Ms Samantha Soulie, the director, wants to know what the training needs of your employees are. You need to interview all your colleagues to gather information for Ms Soulie. Unfortunately, many employees are on holiday and you will not be able to send the information Ms Soulie wants by her preferred deadline (the end of this week). Send an email to Ms Soulie informing her of the delay.

_____

_____

_____

_____

_____

_____

_____

_____

_____

_____

_____

_____

_____

_____

UNIT 11: Assignment 2

You have received two books from Can-o-can-aya Books (Fun Family Holidays and Beating Business Blues) and an invoice for ¥37,500. You do not remember ordering any such books. Send an email to orders@ can-o-can-aya.jp telling them about the problem. You plan to return the books ASAP and you have decided not to pay for them.

_____

_____

_____

_____

_____

_____

_____

_____

_____

_____

_____

_____

_____

_____

UNIT 11: Assignment 3

You have been selected to attend a short leadership program at Vanguard University. There are four programs: Advanced Management Program, General Management Program, Program for Leadership Development, and High Potential Leadership Program.

Contact the program coordinator (Ms Shirlee Ronson) and find out all relevant information to help you decide on which course to pursue.

_____

_____

_____

_____

_____

_____

_____

_____

_____

_____

_____

_____

Unit 12
Writing Frameworks

Writing frameworks are useful for those days when you are pressed for time and you need to write something quickly. A framework gives you a preorganized way to structure your ideas.

Here are some examples:

1. PPF – Past, Present, Future

Let's say your topic is: My work experience

Using PPF you might say something like this:

In the past, that is, when I was in university, I worked part-time as a youth coordinator. In this job, I was responsible for providing advice to a group of young people who had dropped out of school but were thinking of going back. I had to do a lot of research to find the right information for the students. In fact, even though I was supposed to help the students, I ended up benefiting most of all because I learned a great deal about how to do research and find reliable sources.

At present, I am a stock trader. It is a high-pressure job but I love it because it gives me an opportunity to work with analysts and to interview company leaders. Even though I am still relatively young, I get to interact with a lot of experienced people and many of them are generous with advice. I think that all the advice I am receiving will help me in my career over time.

In the future, I would like to go back to school and get another degree. My goal is to teach in the university, possibly in the field of business. I may be able to combine theory with practical business knowledge to help students who aspire to enter the business world. For now, I want to do as well as I can in anything I tackle, but I do not think I will be ready for any kind of major change until after four or five years.

2. PREP

> P - Point
> R - Reason
> E - Example
> P - Point

The PREP framework can be considered a basic paragraph.

Let's say your topic is something as simple as fine dining in Tokyo.

Using PREP, you first make a point, for example, "Tokyo is a mecca for fine dining, and then follow it up with a reason."

> P: Tokyo is a mecca for fine dining.
> R: ...because Tokyo even beats Paris when it comes to the number of Michelin-starred restaurants in the city.
> E: For instance, it is possible to get a wide range of fine food, including French, Italian, and Thai in Tokyo. Some of these restaurants are charming little places — hidden gems, really.
> P: If you are a food lover, as I am, Tokyo is where you need to be to eat your way around the world.

3. The Twist – The Change – The Shift

People change; businesses change; societies change. There are times when you may have to write about such a change in your business, your department, or your life. In such a case, you can write about how things used to be, then mention something that happened to trigger a change (new management, a shocking event, change of policy, etc.), and then go on to the kinds of changes that were made and how successful, or not, those changes may have been.

UNIT 12: Assignment 1

The final meeting for launching your company's NextGen (next generation) services is set to begin in two hours. You have a migraine headache and might not be able to make the presentation that everyone is waiting for! Dash off a quick email to the boss, Mr Wilson Furtado, explaining your condition and predicament.

_____

_____

_____

_____

_____

_____

_____

_____

_____

_____

_____

_____

_____

UNIT 12: Assignment 2

You are going to attend a departmental meeting next week. The chairperson, Ms Junko Haruna, has asked you and others to email suggestions on possible cost cutting in your department. Send your suggestions ASAP to her at: junko.haruna@company.com.

_____

_____

_____

_____

_____

_____

_____

_____

_____

_____

_____

_____

_____

_____

_____

_____

UNIT 12: Assignment 3

Several of your company's customers have been complaining that their concerns are not resolved quickly enough. As a team leader, write to members of your team suggesting ways for the team to be more responsive to the needs of customers.

_____

_____

_____

_____

_____

_____

_____

_____

_____

_____

_____

_____

_____

_____

_____

_____

Unit 13
Relevance

We always have to make choices when we are writing letters, emails, or reports. If we had all the time in the world, we could write endlessly. But how much information do we really need to share? If a brief letter can get you what you need, why write a long letter and waste both your time and the reader's?

On the other hand, if you need to give background information on a subject and you fail to do so, the recipient might write and ask for clarification. That also wastes time. So, consider carefully how much information you need to convey — not too little and certainly not more than is necessary.

Also, as a businessperson, there are times when, for tactical reasons, you do not want to share certain pieces of information with people who are not entitled to such information. Every company has its secrets, including costs, methods, procedures, or internal relationships. Be discreet.

UNIT 13: Assignment 1

Your colleague from the accounting department, Ms Selena Yanase, has invited you and others to go for drinks at Architects Café. You have a lot of work to do and might not be able to attend. Reply.

_____

_____

_____

_____

_____

_____

_____

_____

_____

_____

_____

_____

_____

_____

_____

_____

UNIT 13: Assignment 2

Your colleague from another branch of your company will be visiting the town or city in which you live and wants you to suggest a few must-see places. Reply.

_____

_____

_____

_____

_____

_____

_____

_____

_____

_____

_____

_____

_____

_____

UNIT 13: Assignment 3

You are going on a business trip. Ms Linda Gustano, the secretary, has booked the KitaYogo Hotel for you. You stayed at this hotel before; it was filthy and not a place you care to spend another night. Send an email to Ms Gustano asking that she find another place for you.

_____

_____

_____

_____

_____

_____

_____

_____

_____

_____

_____

_____

_____

_____

Unit 14
From IDAC to GIDAC

Using IDAC, you can write emails that are straight to the point and businesslike. If all of your emails are like that, however, some of the people you deal with might feel that you lack warmth. After you have been in contact with someone for a while, it is only natural that you show that the relationship has evolved. In this regard, you have to pay close attention to cues from the other person. Some people do not want to be too friendly with their business associates or colleagues. Others expect that after you've got to know them a little better, you will be somewhat friendly towards them. Here's an example of a letter that opens with a greeting.

Dear Jay,

Greeting   Hope you are having a great day.

Introduction   I have located the report on medical waste that you requested last week.

Details   We do not have a soft copy of the text so I am going to scan the pages and send them to you later on today.

Action   Meanwhile, if you have any other request, please let me know as soon as possible.

Closing   I look forward to chatting with you shortly.

Sincerely,
Saleem Bubakar
Senior Engineer

Think Carefully About Your Greeting

In order to get the greeting right, think about who you are writing to.

Do you already have a business relationship with this person? What is the person's rank? Is it alright to open with a casual greeting? Or would a greeting that is a little more formal be preferable? Don't write long, rambling greetings. Keep your greetings short but warm.

UNIT 14: Assignment 1

The big dictionary on the shelf near your desk has gone missing over the past two weeks. You are wondering if someone borrowed it and forgot to return it. You like that dictionary a lot and you would like to see it returned ASAP. Send an email to all employees in your branch.

_____

_____

_____

_____

_____

_____

_____

_____

_____

_____

_____

_____

_____

UNIT 14: Assignment 2

Your company has set up a series of evening courses for employees to improve negotiation skills (three hours/three nights a week). The so-called 3-3-3 (Triple Three) program will run for three weeks. You would like to see some changes made to the program because you and your colleagues are usually too tired after work to benefit fully from the program. Send an email to HR head, Mr K. Yamada, with your suggestions for change to the program.

_____

_____

_____

_____

_____

_____

_____

_____

_____

_____

_____

_____

_____

UNIT 14: Assignment 3

You are working on a presentation and need help with creating some special charts. Mr Eli Yamamura might be able to help you pull it off. Send him an urgent message asking for his assistance.

Unit 15
Good News and Bad News Letters

Businesses send out many routine letters: asking about another company's services, for example. In such cases, the IDAC formula works well. State the purpose of the letter upfront, give the reader a brief background, include an action item, and then, close.

IDAC (for routine and positive letters)

I: **Introduction** (main point – request for services; congratulations, etc.)

D: **Details** (explanation, reasons, background)

A: **Action** (what you expect or plan to do: meeting, phone call, delivery, etc.)

C: **Close**

For bad news letters, however, it is not a good idea to get straight to the point. You do not want to shock the recipient or reader. As such, you begin by presenting a buffer, that is, information that is neutral or positive. This will relax the reader and help serve as a lead-in to the bad news. When you deliver the bad news, please don't go into too much detail. You can soften the impact of the blow by not exaggerating the problem. Rather, you can offer another buffer after you present the bad news, and then go on to a brief close.

BDBC: Negative situations

B: Buffer (say something that would soften the impact of the coming bad news)

D: Details (explain or give the negative news)

B: Buffer (give another piece of information to soften the impact)

C: Close (end pleasantly and briefly)

Sample letter

Dear James Takara,

B: Your application for the position of purchasing assistant was carefully reviewed by our management.

D: We regret to inform you that the position has been filled by another candidate.

B: We were very much impressed by the breadth of your experience and would, therefore, like to keep your resume on file should a suitable position open up in the future.

C: We wish you all the very best in all your future endeavors.

Sincerely,

Taka Nakamaru
Managing Director, Purchasing

UNIT 15: Assignment 1

Ms Wendy Wexlinks applied for your company's Preferred Client Status Card. This card is given to very few people, usually those who have proven themselves loyal to the company for many years. The card comes with a number of perks such as free use of resorts and spas worldwide. Write to Ms Wexlinks and inform her of the approval of her application.

_____

_____

_____

_____

_____

_____

_____

_____

_____

_____

_____

_____

_____

_____

UNIT 15: Assignment 2

Mr Jimmy Hope sent you a fax: "Hello. Our printing company has installed new machines. Really good ones too. We know you have a big printing job coming up. We would really like you to offer us this job. We'll do a helluva job for you. And by the way, we need the business! Thanks."

You have been asked to reply to Mr Hope. The reality is that the large printing order has been offered to another company. You do not have any other printing jobs coming up any time soon.

_____

_____

_____

_____

_____

_____

_____

_____

_____

_____

_____

_____

_____

UNIT 15: Assignment 3

Your company is considering setting up a flexible work schedule to encourage greater work-life balance. Before its implementation, however, management would like to know what each employee thinks of this idea. Email rika.honda@company.com with your views.

_____

_____

_____

_____

_____

_____

_____

_____

_____

_____

_____

_____

_____

_____

_____

_____

Unit 16
Grammatically Correct Writing

The non-native speaker who can speak grammatically correct English earns a great deal of respect. English grammar has many areas of uncertainty even for native speakers and there are many points of grammar that continue to be debated among the most learned in the English speaking world.

But your goal may not be to become a grammarian; you may just want to be able to write well enough to be understood. Bad grammar, including lack of proper punctuation, could result in misunderstanding.

If you want to be an effective business writer, you cannot afford to ignore grammar.

Grammar books sell well because many language learners recognize the importance of grammar. But once the book gets home, how often do we take the time to study it? It really does not help that many grammar books seem to try so very hard to be boring!

Still, if you are serious about improving your writing skills, you have to steel yourself to go through, not one, but several grammar books. This is because some grammar books explain some concepts better than others. So, by going through different grammar books, you may increase your chances of really getting to understand some of the more challenging areas of grammar.

Another way of improving your grammar is to become an avid reader. After all, most good writers admit to reading extensively.

UNIT 16: Assignment 1

You have been informed by HR that because of your excellent work performance, you are being sent to another country for three years. You absolutely do not want to go for various reasons. You want to tell HR: "No way!!!"

UNIT 16: Assignment 2

Your friend has complained to you that her boss always asks for her advice, but never follows the advice. She is getting irritated that the boss is wasting her time. You have some words of advice for your friend.

_____

_____

_____

_____

_____

_____

_____

_____

_____

_____

_____

_____

_____

_____

_____

UNIT 16: Assignment 3

Your family member is seriously sick and you are the only person available to take care of her. Send an email to your boss requesting three days off.

_____

_____

_____

_____

_____

_____

_____

_____

_____

_____

_____

_____

_____

_____

_____

_____

Additional Writing Tasks

Assignment 1

You are the boss. Times are hard and you are forced to do the unthinkable: reduce employee salaries. You think this will be temporary and you find no joy in having to do it but the company may not survive otherwise. Send an email to all employees informing them about the company's current situation and the plan you have come up with to keep the company afloat.

_____

_____

_____

_____

_____

_____

_____

_____

_____

_____

_____

Assignment 2

A former employee, Ms Sayaha Balbadur, has asked you to write a letter of recommendation extolling her professional virtues, experience and contributions to your firm. Write the letter with the following attention line: To Whom It May Concern

_____

_____

_____

_____

_____

_____

_____

_____

_____

_____

_____

_____

_____

_____

_____

Assignment 3

You recently interviewed two applicants for a position in your company. You were impressed with the overall background and skills of both applicants. Unfortunately, there was room for only one hire. Send an email to the applicant who was not hired.

_____

_____

_____

_____

_____

_____

_____

_____

_____

_____

_____

_____

_____

_____

_____

Assignment 4

You are inspired by the accomplishments of scientists – their dedication, willpower, curiosity, and willingness to collaborate with others. You want employees in your company to develop similar qualities. Write an email to a Nobel Prize winner of your choice and invite her to give the keynote address at your company's end-of-year function.

_____

_____

_____

_____

_____

_____

_____

_____

_____

_____

_____

_____

_____

Assignment 5

Your company has a bright idea to get employees to work only four days a week by stretching the workday from 8 am to 8 pm, with a one-hour break between 12 noon and 1 pm. You are not thrilled about the idea and want to discourage the company from carrying it out. Write to the president, Ms Youngsan Park, about your concerns.

References

Buffett, Warren. Annual Report 2006. Berkshire Hathaway.

Interviews. Ernest Hemingway, The Art of Fiction, No. 21, *The Paris Review*
www.parisreview.org

Taylor, Shirley. Model Business Letters, E-mails & Other Business
Books. 6th Edition. Pitman Publishing Co., 2003

Recommended Books

Bradbury, Ray. Zen in the Art of Writing. New York: Bantam, 1992.

Burchfield, Robert William, ed. The new Fowler's modern English usage. No. RD C10 10. Oxford: Clarendon Press, 1996.

Flesch, Rudolf Franz. "Art of readable writing." (1949).

Flesch, Rudolf. "The art of clear thinking." (1951).

Schrampfer Azar, Betty. "Understanding and using English grammar." Published by Binarupa Aksara (1999).

Strunk, William. The elements of style. Penguin, 2007.

Swan, Michael. Practical english usage. No. 425 S926P 1995.. New-York, 1992.

Waddell, Marie L. The art of styling sentences: 20 patterns for success. Barron's Educational Series, 1993.

* These are just suggestions to give you an idea of the kind of books you should look for if you are eager to improve your writing and grammar.

About the Author

Everett Ofori holds an MBA from Heriot-Watt University (Scotland, UK). He teaches Public Speaking, Management, Marketing, and English for Specific Purposes (Business Writing, Medical Writing, Meeting Facilitation, etc.). He has worked extensively with business executives (including those at the C-level) but is equally at home with helping young people hone their writing skills or become more effective in expressing themselves verbally. Everett has helped hundreds of high school and university students around the world to improve their writing and grades.

Everett has worked with clients/students from the following organizations and more:

• Accenture	• Actelion
• Asahi Kasei Medical	• Asahi Soft Drink Research, Moriya
• AXA	• Barclays
• Becton Dickinson	• Boston Consulting
• Coca Cola	• Deutsche Bank
• Disney Japan	• ExxonMobil
• Fujitsu	• Goldman Sachs
• Hitachi Automotive	• Hitachi Design
• IIJ (Internet Initiative Japan)	• Johnson & Johnson (Janssen)
• McKinsey Japan	• Mitsubishi (Shoji)
• Mizuho Bank	• Moody's
• National Institute of Land and Infrastructure Management, Tsukuba, Japan (NILIM)	• Nomura
• Orix	• PriceWaterhouseCoopers (PWC)
• Recruit	• Reinsurance Group of America (RGA - Japan)
• Sekizenkai Nursing School, Shimosoga, Kanagawa	• Sumitomo
• Summit Agro International	• Suntory
• Tokyo International Business College, Asakusabashi, Tokyo	• Yahoo (Gyao)
• Yokogawa Meters and Instruments	• Yokohama Child Welfare Vocational College (Hoiku Fukushi), Higashi Totsuka, Kanagawa

Notes